A

b

FUN PHONICS
Upper and lower case alphabet

3 - 6 Years

Activity Centre

c

D

First published in 2017 by The Activity Centre Pty Ltd.
2 West Street, Pascoe Vale, Victoria, 3044 Australia
www.theactivitycentre.com.au

Written by Nilhara Perumal
Copyright © 2017 The Activity Centre Pty Ltd.

ISBN: 978-0-6480563-2-4

Find out about the other Activity Centre books and educational materials:
www.theactivitycentre.com.au

This book belongs to

_____

Draw yourself in the circle

Let's Start!

Welcome to The Activity Centre

A key philosophy of The Activity Centre is that "a child is only small in size". We place importance on what children "can" do rather than what they cannot do.

The Activity Centre materials are designed to encourage children to develop their own identity and find their own voice from the earliest age.

Fun Phonics is a wonderful book for children aged between 3–6 years.

To start, it is important that a child learns how to hold a pencil. A groove pencil or pencil grips may help master this skill.

Once your child is able to hold a pencil and draw basic shapes, they are ready to start printing the alphabet.

This book focuses on upper and lower case letters of the alphabet, allowing children to develop essential reading and writing skills.

Always give your child lots of encouragement and praise, and remember, the stars at the bottom of each activity are a reward for their awesome effort and achievement.

Let's practice using a pencil. Trace the lines and shapes below.

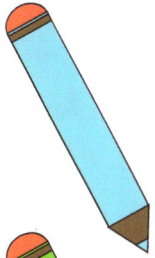

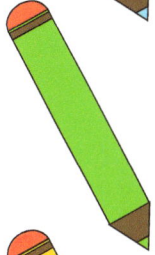

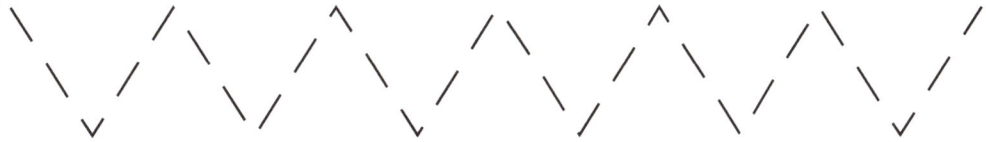

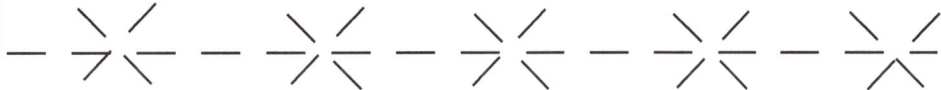

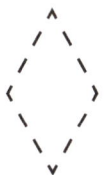

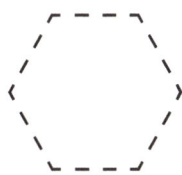

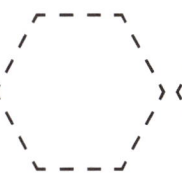

# Aa  Aa for apple	# Bb  Bb for ball	# Cc  Cc for cat	# Dd  Dd for dolphin	# Ee  Ee for elephant
# Ff  Ff for fish	# Gg  Gg for guitar	# Hh  Hh for hop	# Ii  Ii for ink	# Jj  Jj for jellyfish
# Kk  Kk for kite	# Ll 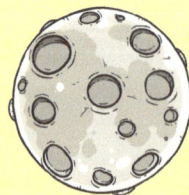 Ll for lollipop	# Mm 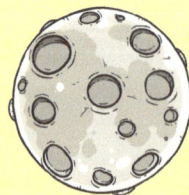 Mm for moon	# Nn  Nn for nest	# Oo  Oo for octopus

# Pp  Pp for pig	# Qq  Qq for queen	# Rr  Rr for rain	# Ss  Ss for snake	# Tt  Tt for turtle
# Uu  Uu for umbrella	# Vv  Vv for van	# Ww  Ww for watch	# Xx  Xx for x-ray	# Yy  Yy for yoyo
# Zz  Zz for zipper				

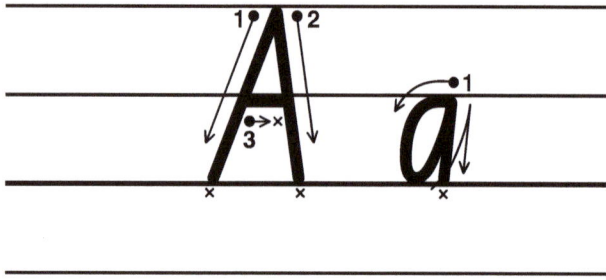

Aa for apple

Let's practice. Trace and write the letters.

Let's start to read: each word begins with 'A'.

| Ant | Arm | Aeroplane |

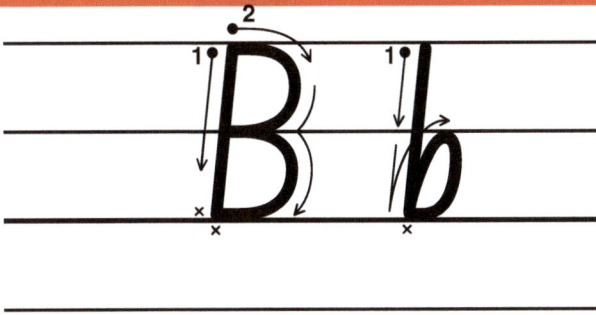

B b

Bb for banana

Let's practice. Trace and write the letters.

B B B B B B B B

B B

b b b b b b

Let's start to read: each word begins with 'B'.

Ball	Bee	Book

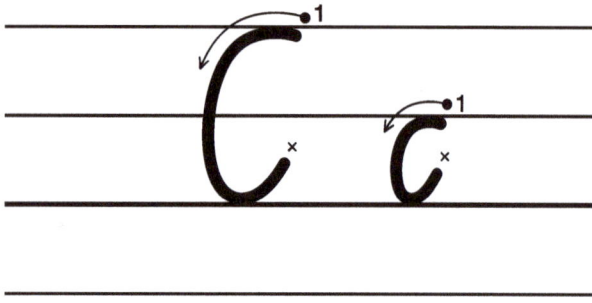

Cc for carrot

Let's practice. Trace and write the letters.

Let's start to read: each word begins with 'C'.

Car	Cloud	Cake

Dd for dog

Let's practice. Trace and write the letters.

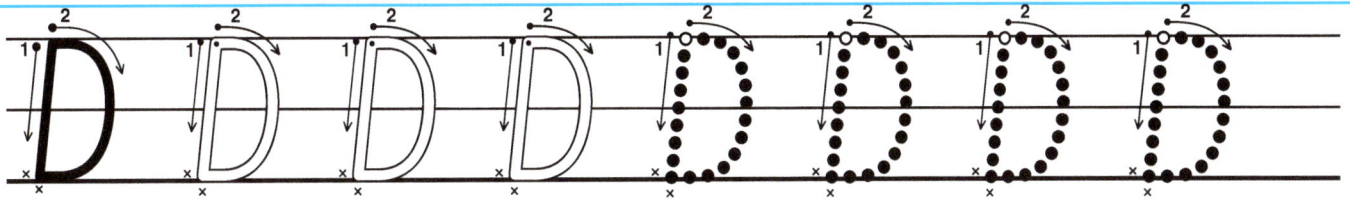

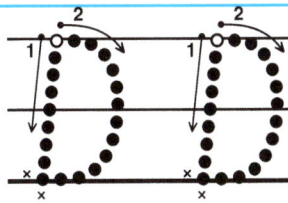

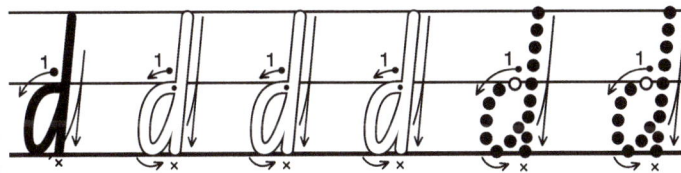

Let's start to read: each word begins with 'D'.

Doughnut	Dolphin	Drum

Join the upper case and lower case letters to the correct picture.

A

B

C

D

c

d

b

a

How did you do? Colour the stars to show how well you did.

☆ ☆ ☆ ☆

Look at each of the pictures below and circle the letter that each picture begins with.

A   b   d

a   d   b

D   B   A

c   B   a

A   B   c

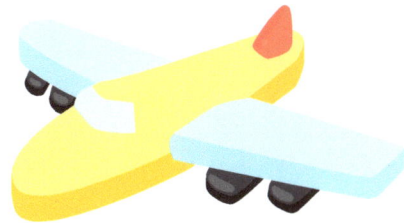

a   d   C

C   d   a

D   C   B

How did you do? Colour the stars to show how well you did.

Find the hidden word. Using the pictures, write the correct letter in the boxes below.

The hidden word is ....? Hint???

The hidden word is ....? Hint???

How did you do? Colour the stars to show how well you did.

Let's practice. Trace and write the letters.

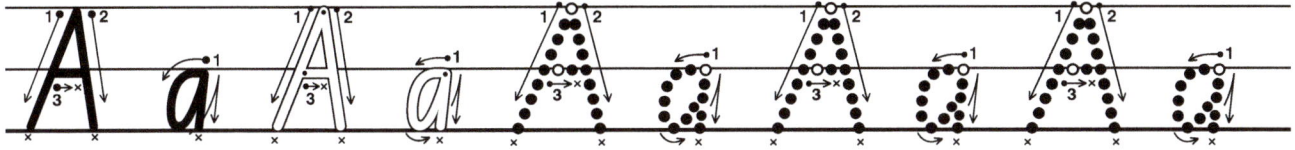

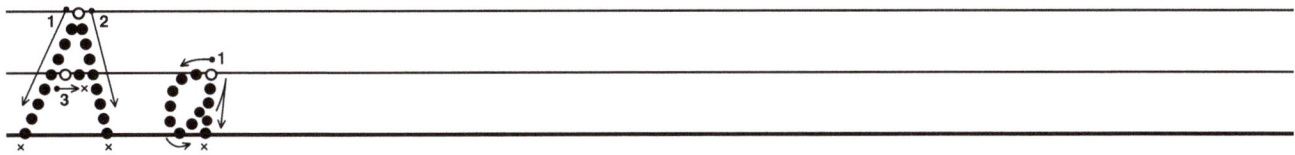

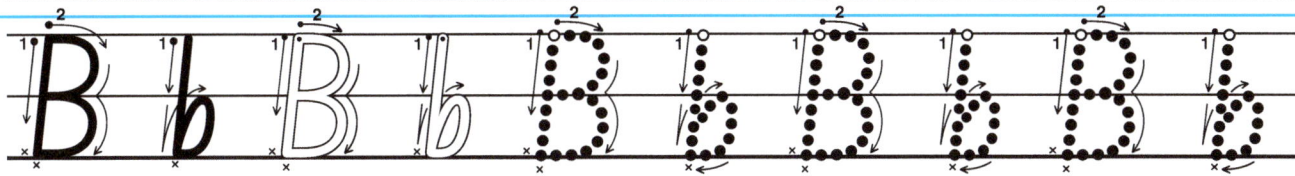

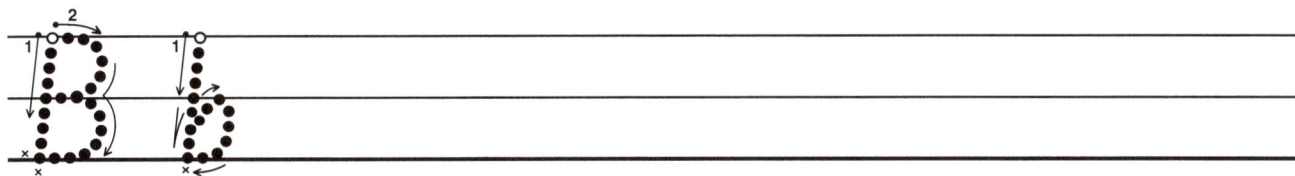

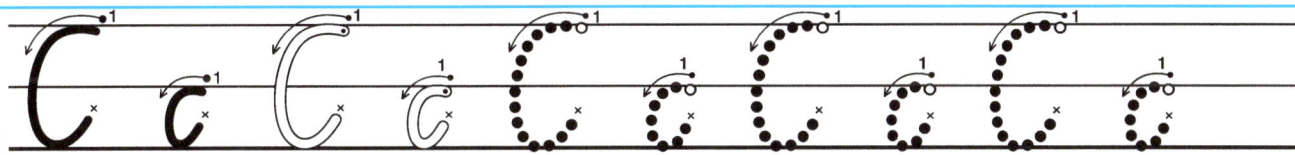

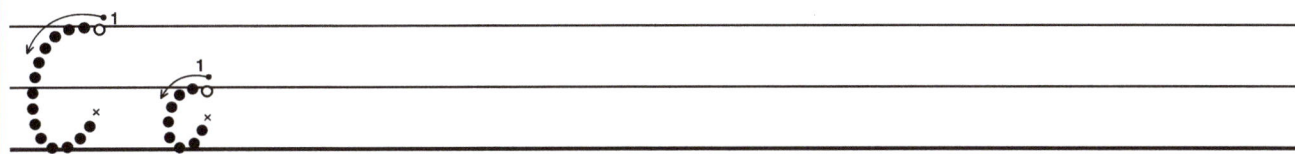

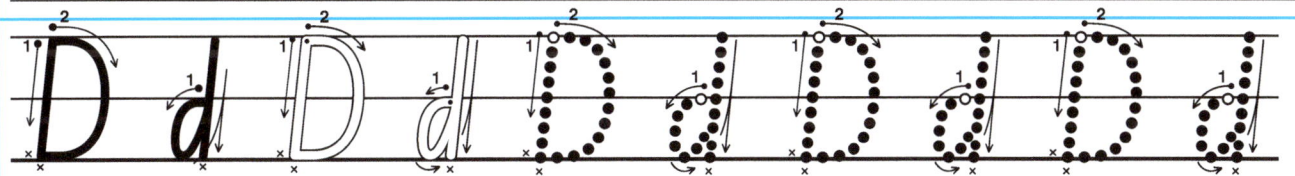

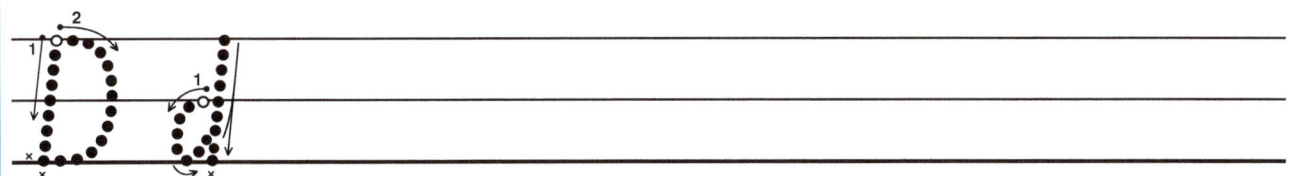

A a A a A a A a A a A a A a

A a

B b B b B b B b B b B b B b

B b

C c C c C c C c C c C c

C c

D d D d D d D d D d D d D d

D d

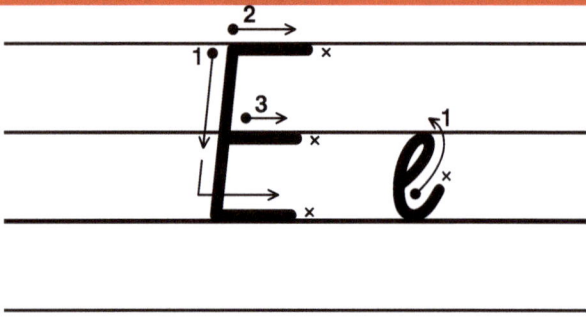

Ee for elephant

Let's practice. Trace and write the letters.

E E E E E E E E E

E E

e e e e e e

Let's start to read: each word begins with 'E'.

Egg	Earth	Eagle

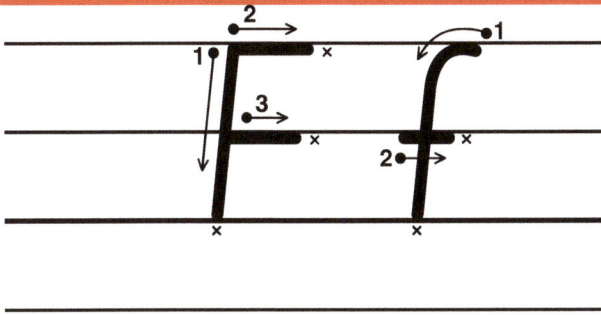

Ff for frog

Let's practice. Trace and write the letters.

Let's start to read: each word begins with 'F'.

Fish	Flower	Fork

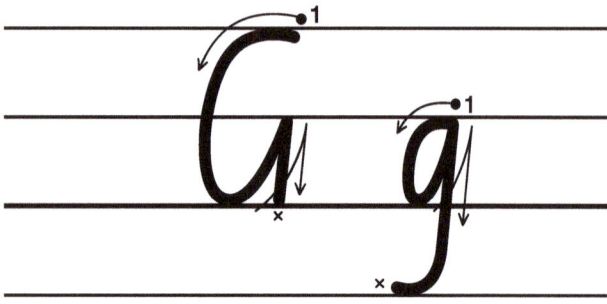

Gg for grasshopper

Let's practice. Trace and write the letters.

Let's start to read: each word begins with 'G'.

Grapes	Giraffe	Guitar

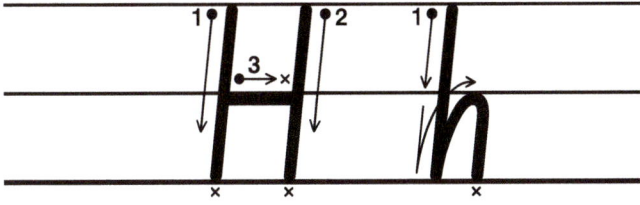

Hh for hop

Let's practice. Trace and write the letters.

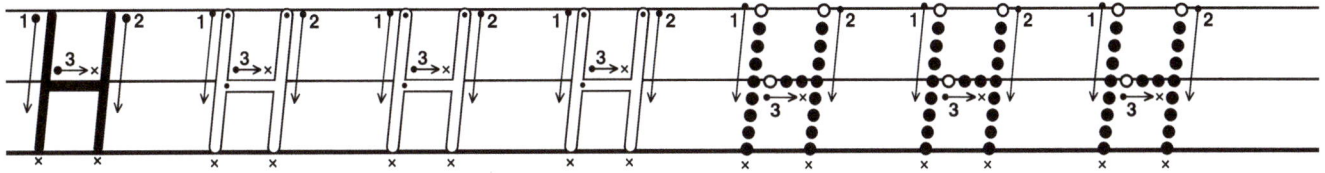

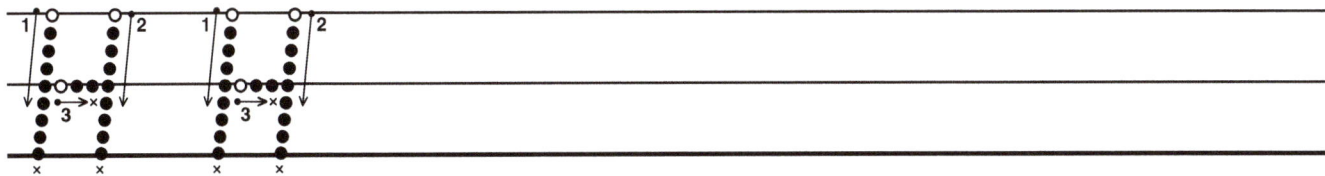

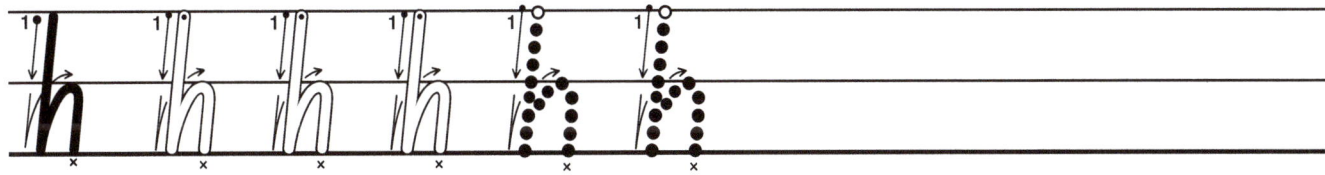

Let's start to read: each word begins with 'H'.

| Hippopotamus | Hand | Heart |

Join the upper case and lower case letters to the correct picture.

E  g

F  h

G  f

H  e

How did you do? Colour the stars to show how well you did.

Look at each of the pictures below and circle the letter that each picture begins with.

e   g   h

E   H   f

G   H   E

F   g   H

f   E   g

G   e   h

e   H   F

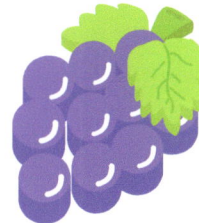

E   G   f

How did you do? Colour the stars to show how well you did.

Find the hidden word. Using the pictures, write the correct letter in the boxes below.

The hidden word is ....? **Hint???**

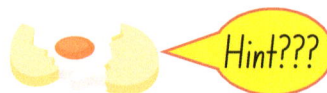

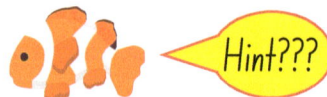

The hidden word is ....? **Hint???**

How did you do? Colour the stars to show how well you did.

Let's practice. Trace and write the letters.

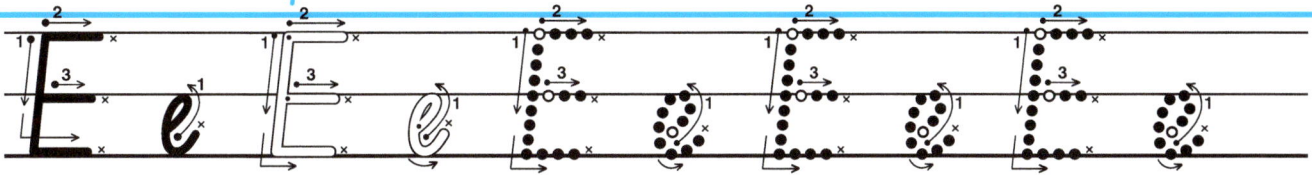

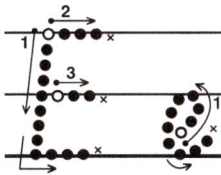

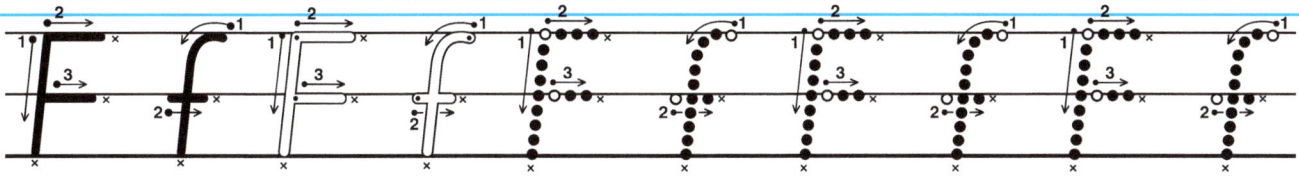

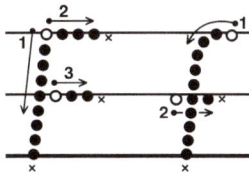

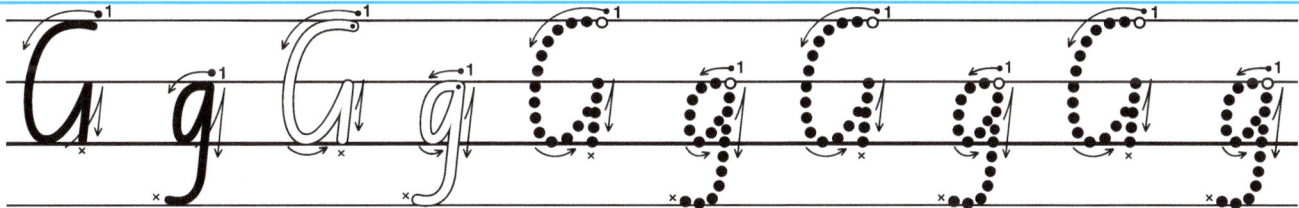

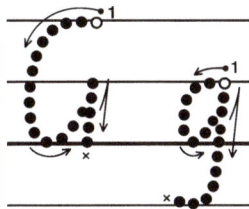

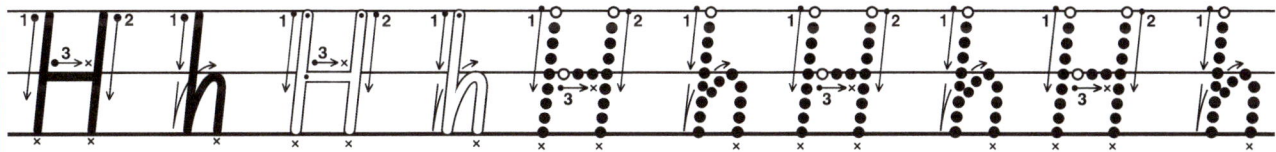

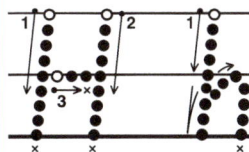

E e E e E e E e E e E e E e E e

E e

F f F f F f F f F f F f F f F f

F f

G g G g G g G g G g G g G g

G g

H h H h H h H h H h H h H h H h

H h

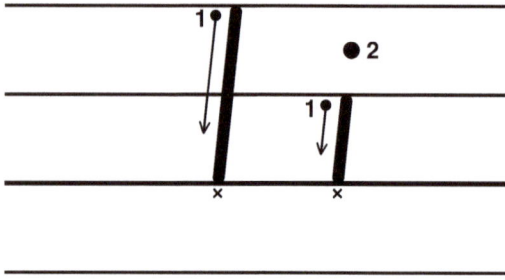

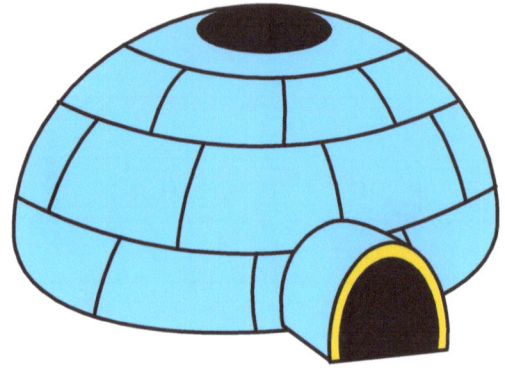

Ii for igloo

Let's practice. Trace and write the letters.

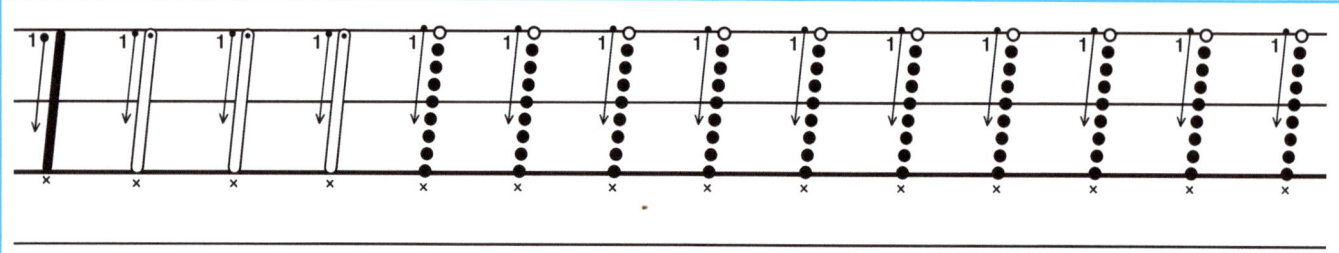

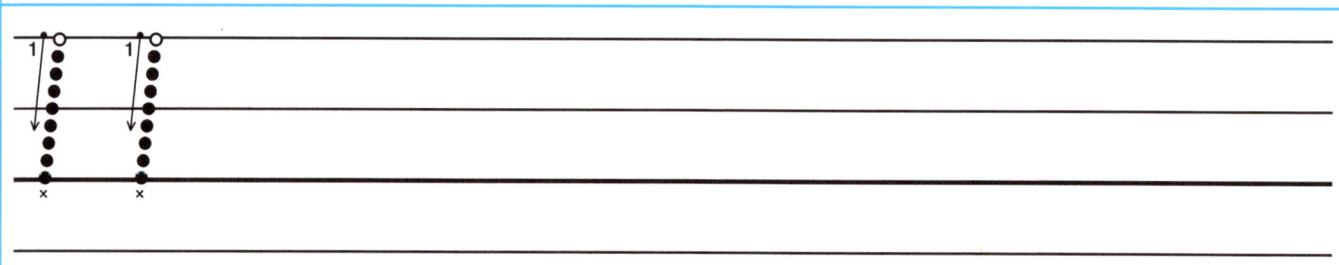

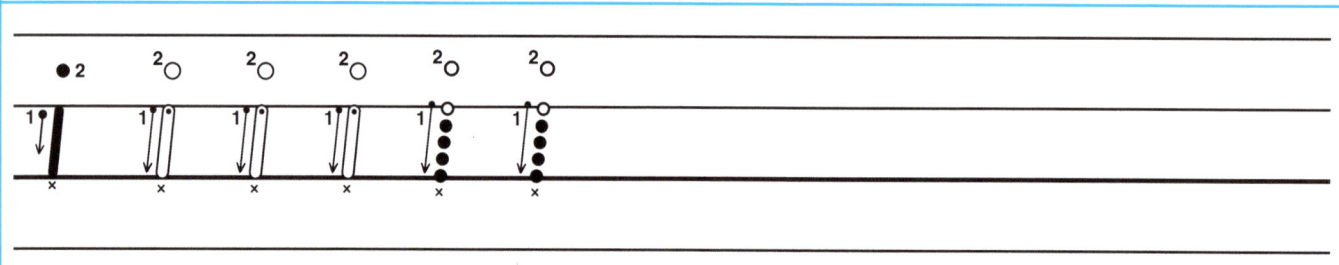

Let's start to read: each word begins with 'I'.

Ice	Ice-cream	Ink

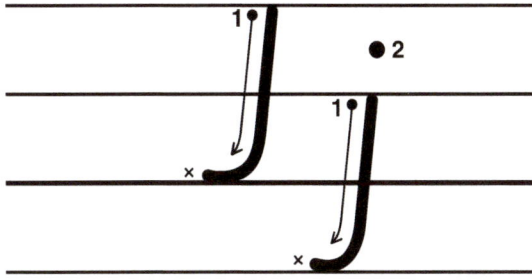

Jj for jug

Let's practice. Trace and write the letters.

Let's start to read: each word begins with 'J'.

Jigsaw	Jam	Jelly

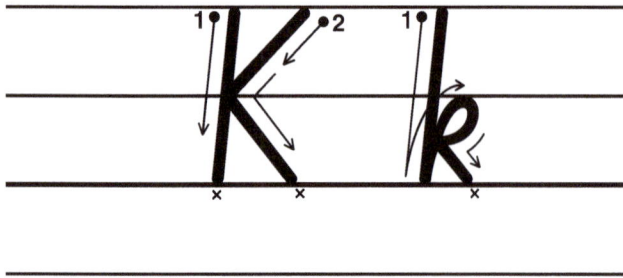

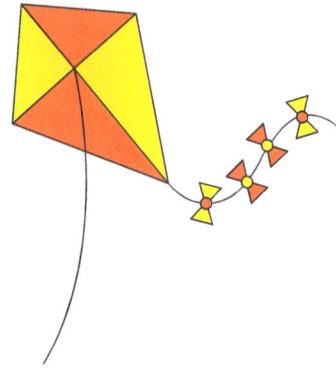

Kk for kite

Let's practice. Trace and write the letters.

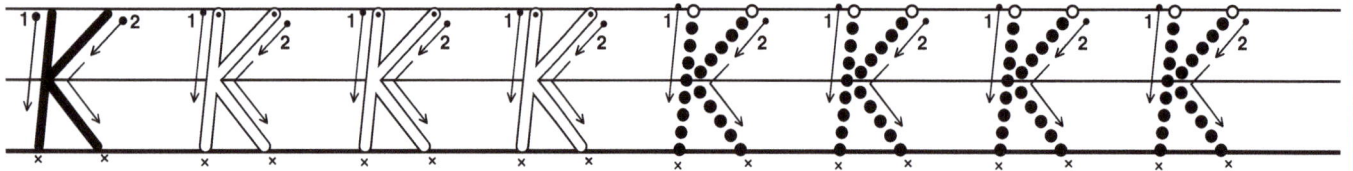

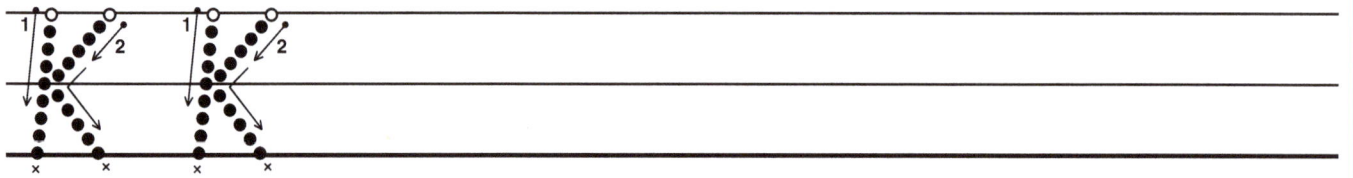

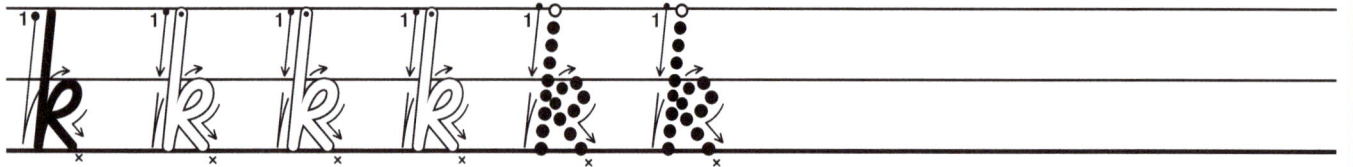

Let's start to read: each word begins with 'K'.

Koala	Key	Kangaroo

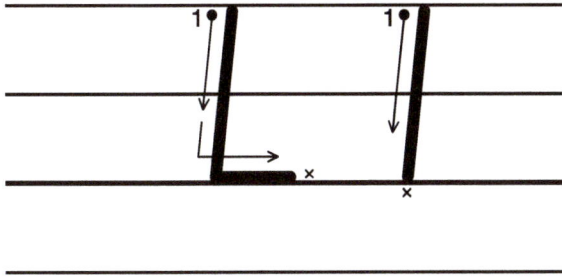

LI for lion

Let's practice. Trace and write the letters.

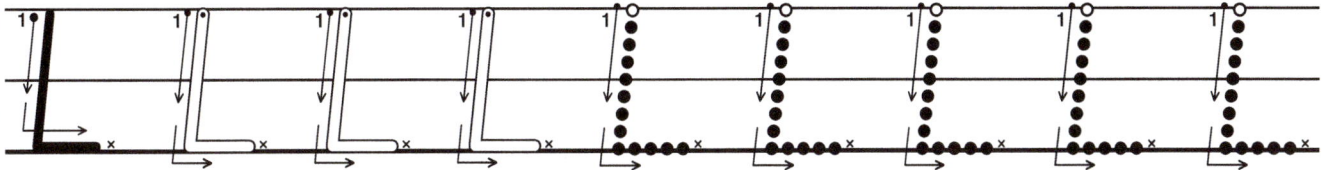

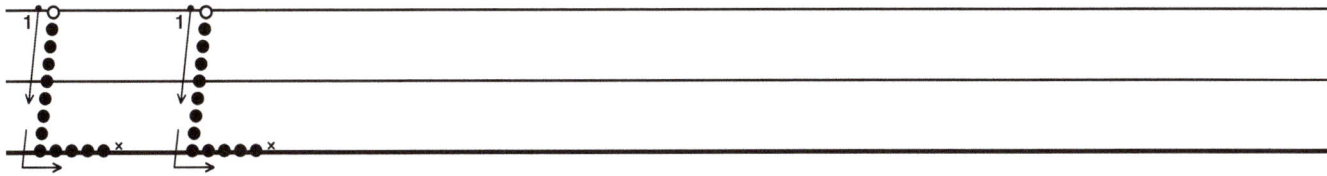

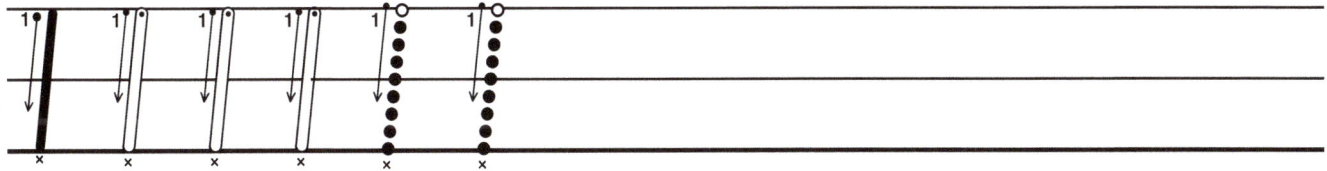

Let's start to read: each word begins with 'L'.

Leaf	Ladybird	Lemon

Join the upper case and lower case letters to the correct picture.

I

k

J

l

K

i

L

j

How did you do? Colour the stars to show how well you did.

Look at each of the pictures below and circle the
letter that each picture begins with.

i k l

L k j

l j K

l L i

J i k

L j K

J l i

j i k

How did you do? Colour the stars to show how well you did.

Find the hidden word. Using the pictures, write the correct letter in the boxes below.

The hidden word is ....? **Hint???**

The hidden word is ....? **Hint???**

How did you do? Colour the stars to show how well you did.

Let's practice. Trace and write the letters.

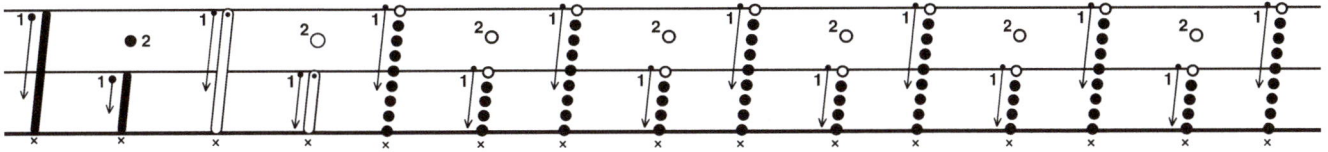

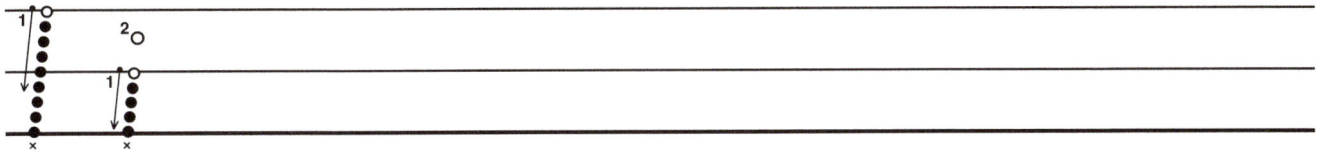

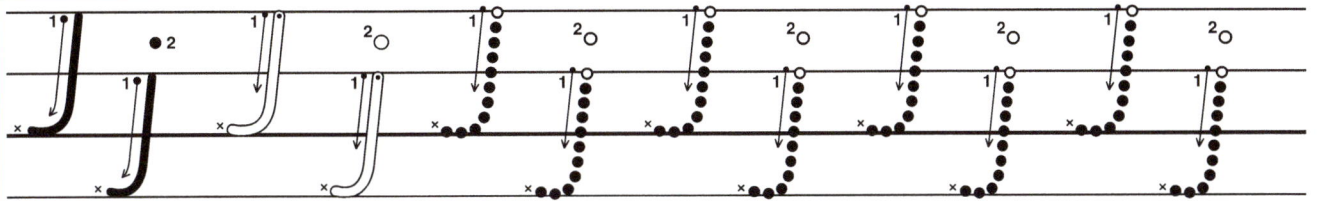

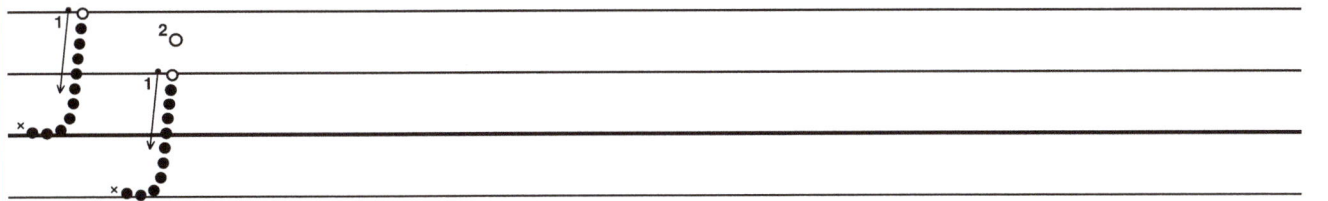

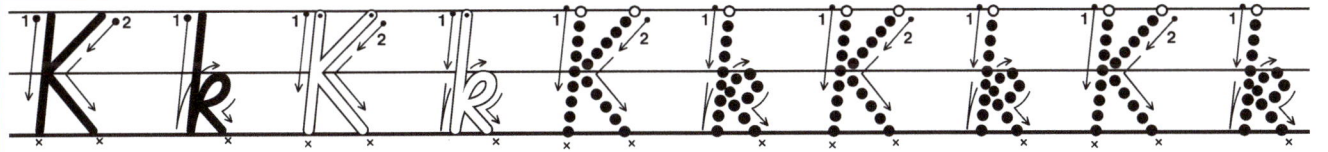

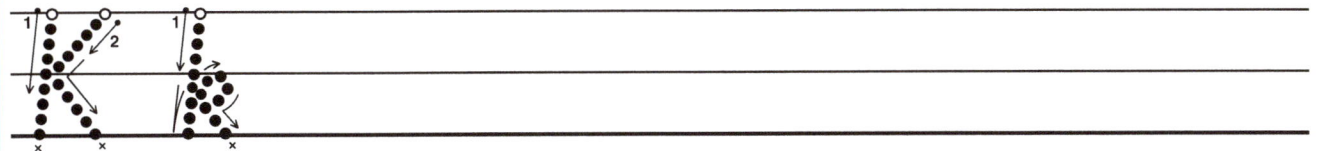

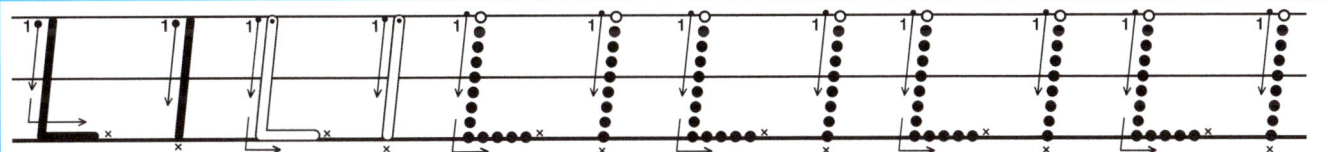

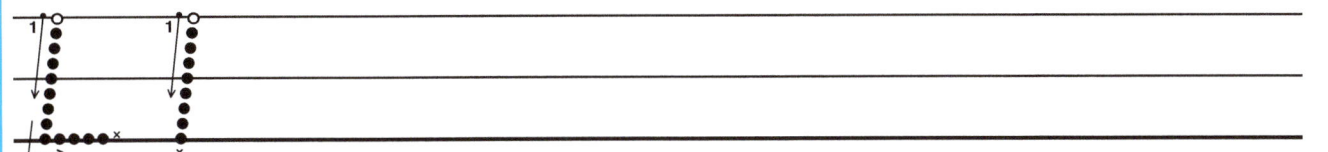

I i

J j

K k

L l

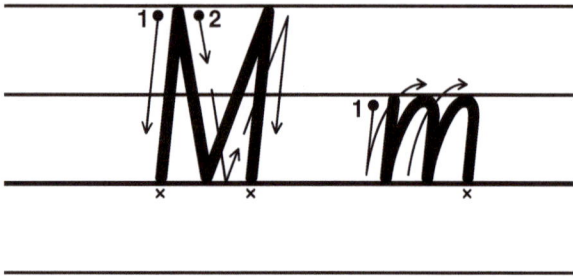

Mm

Mm for monkey

Let's practice. Trace and write the letters.

M M M M M M M

M M

m m m m m m

Let's start to read: each word begins with 'M'.

Moon	Milk	Mushroom

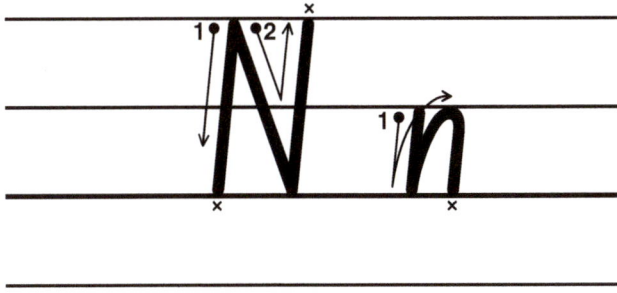

Nn for nest

Let's practice. Trace and write the letters.

Let's start to read: each word begins with 'N'.

Nail	Necklace	Nuts

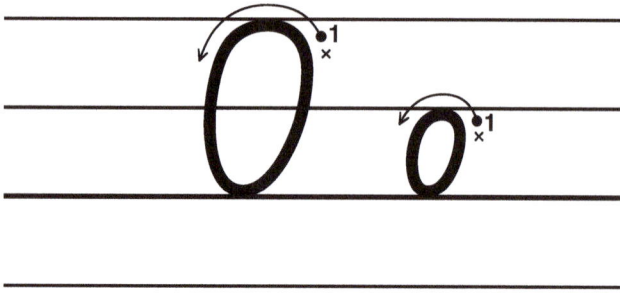

O o

Oo for octopus

Let's practice. Trace and write the letters.

O O O O O O O O

O O

O O O O O O

Let's start to read: each word begins with 'O'.

Owl	Orange	Ostrich

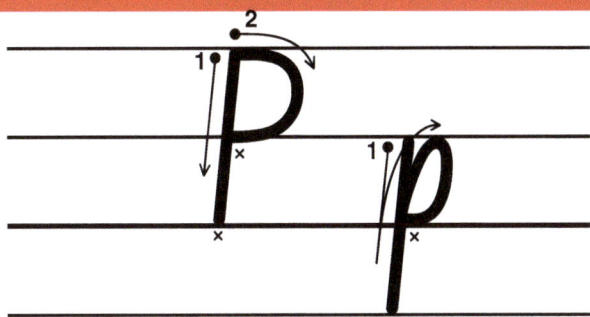

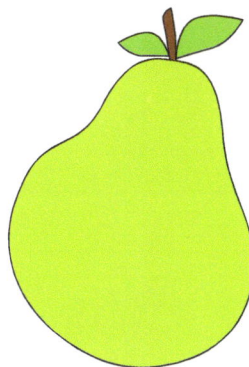

P p

Pp for pear

Let's practice. Trace and write the letters.

P P P P P P P P P P

P P

p p p p p p

Let's start to read: each word begins with 'P'.

Pig	Pencil	Penguin

Join the upper case and lower case letters to the correct picture.

M  o

N  p

P  m

O  n

How did you do? Colour the stars to show how well you did.

Look at each of the pictures below and circle the letter that each picture begins with.

 m P o	 n p M
 P N o	 M O p
 n O m	 o N p
 P m O	 M N P

How did you do? Colour the stars to show how well you did.

Find the hidden word. Using the pictures, write the correct letter in the boxes below.

The hidden word is ....? Hint???

The hidden word is ....? Hint???

How did you do? Colour the stars to show how well you did.

Let's practice. Trace and write the letters.

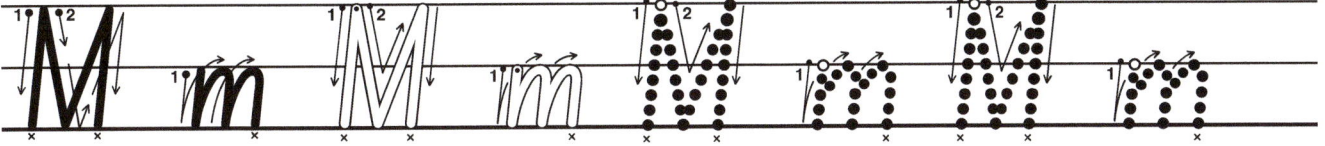

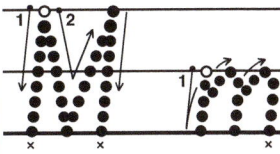

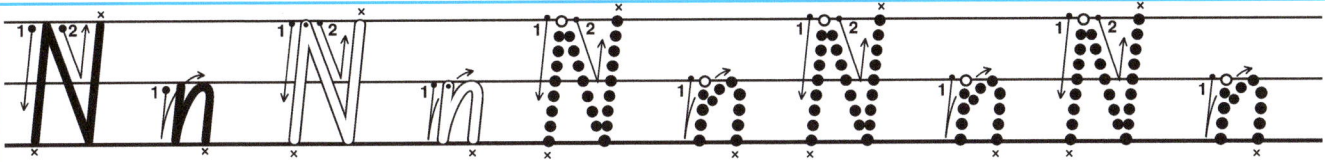

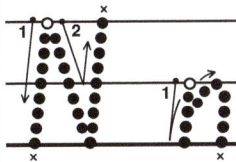

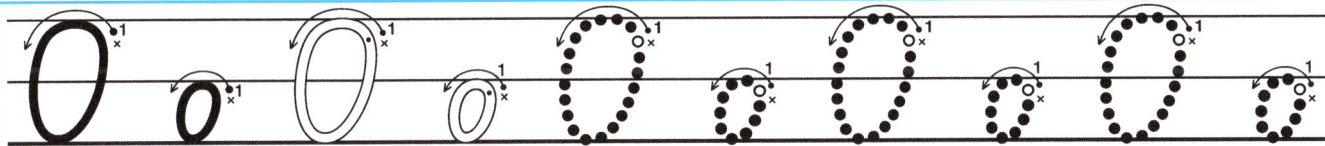

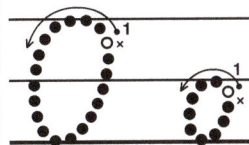

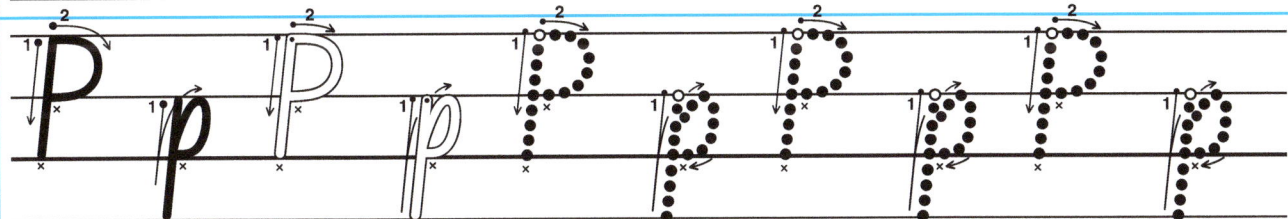

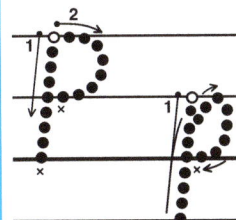

M m M m M m M m

N n N n N n N n

O o O o O o O o

P p P p P p P p

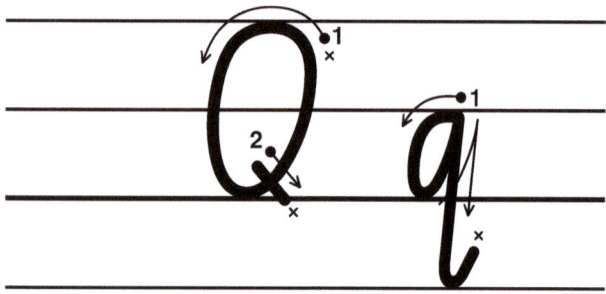

Qq for queen

Let's practice. Trace and write the letters.

Let's start to read: each word begins with 'Q'.

Question	Quill	Quail

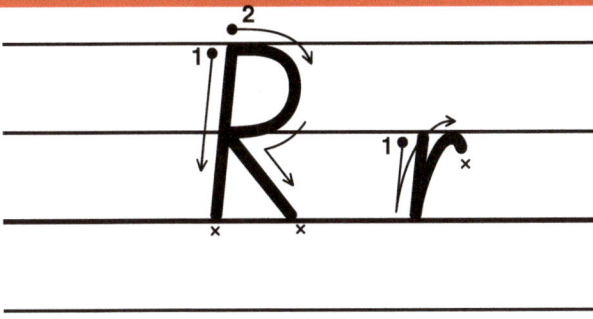

Rr for rocket

Let's practice. Trace and write the letters.

R R R R R R R R R R R

R R

r r r r r r

Let's start to read: each word begins with 'R'.

Rabbit	Ring	Rainbow

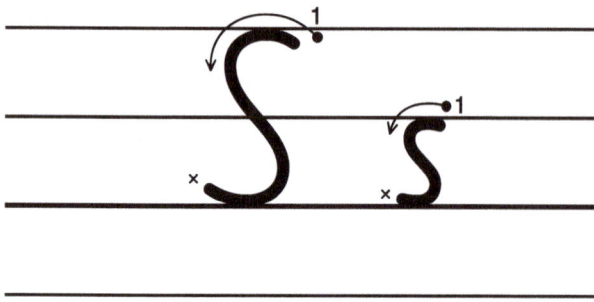

S s

Ss for snake

S S S S S S S S

S S

S S S S S S

Let's start to read: each word begins with 'S'.

| Sun | Strawberry | Snail |

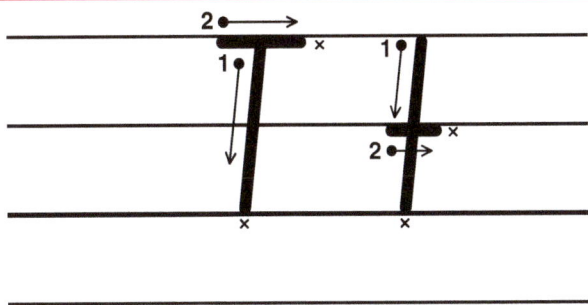

Tt for train

Let's practice. Trace and write the letters.

Let's start to read: each word begins with 'T'.

Tiger	Tennis	Tree

Join the upper case and lower case letters to the correct picture.

Q  t

R  q

S  r

T  s

How did you do? Colour the stars to show how well you did.

Look at each of the pictures below and circle the letter that each picture begins with.

q S t

a Q r

T s Q

t q R

S T r

q r s

t q R

R s Q

How did you do? Colour the stars to show how well you did.

Find the hidden word. Using the pictures, write the correct letter in the boxes below.

The hidden word is ....? Hint???

The hidden word is ....? Hint???

How did you do? Colour the stars to show how well you did.

Let's practice. Trace and write the letters.

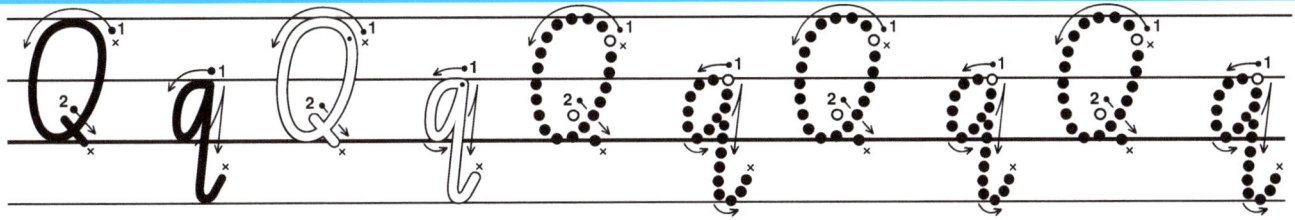

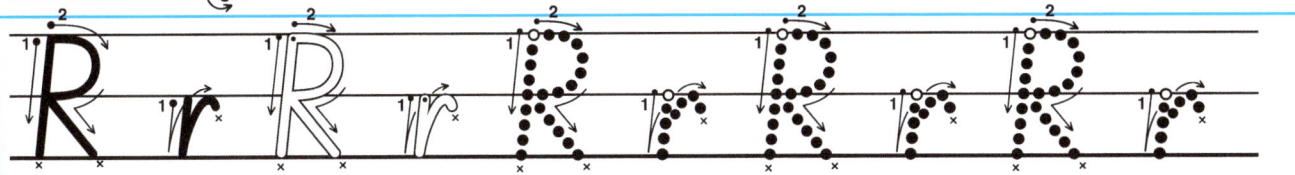

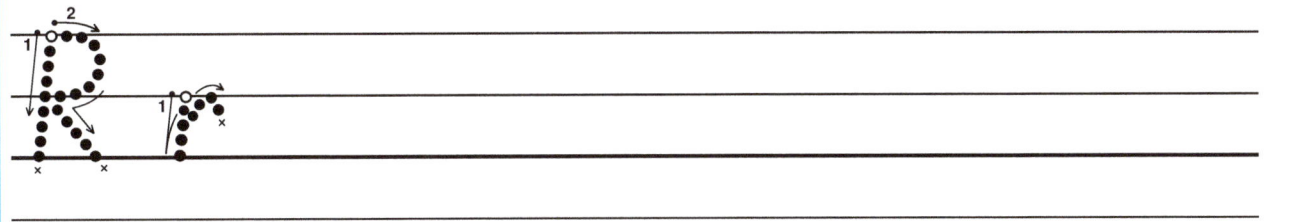

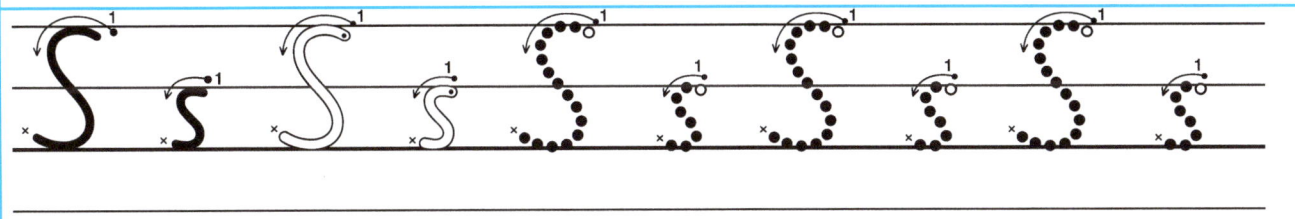

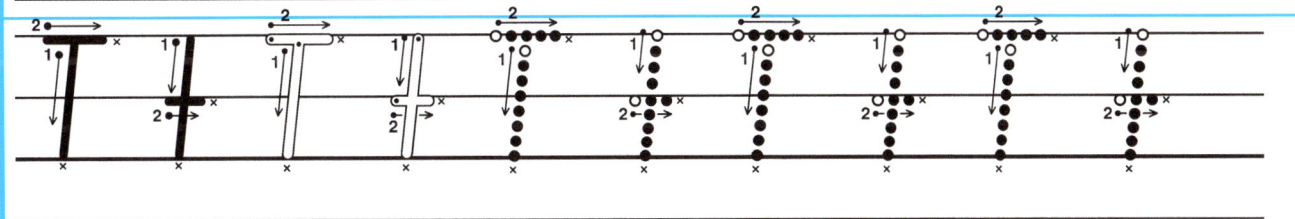

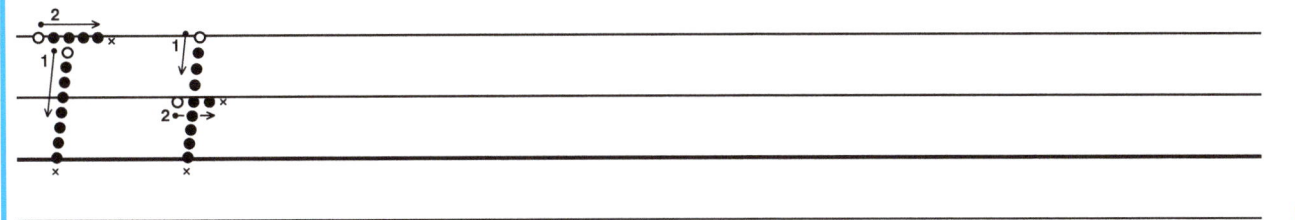

Qq Qq Qq Qq Qq Qq

Qq

Rr Rr Rr Rr Rr Rr

Rr

Ss Ss Ss Ss Ss Ss

Ss

Tt Tt Tt Tt Tt Tt

Tt

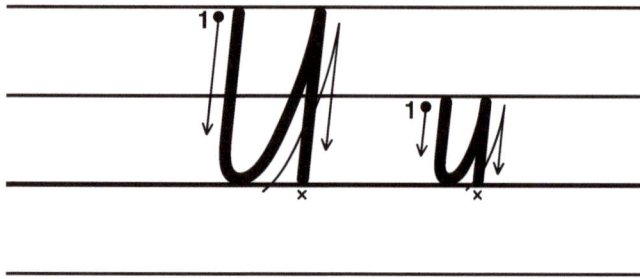

Uu for umbrella

Let's practice. Trace and write the letters.

Let's start to read: each word begins with 'U'.

Unlock	Unicorn	UFO

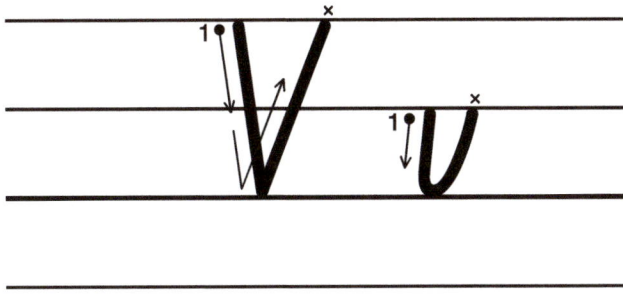

Vu for violin

Let's practice. Trace and write the letters.

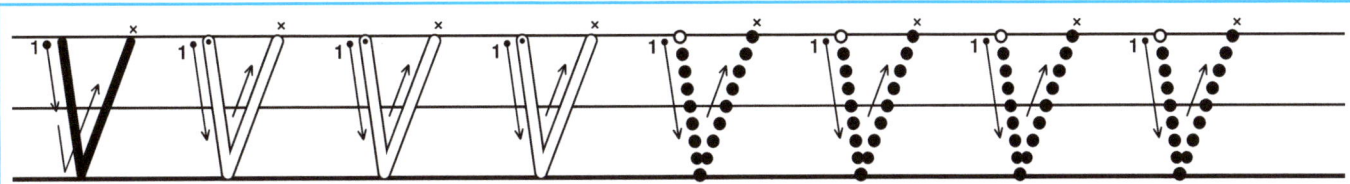

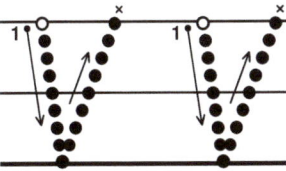

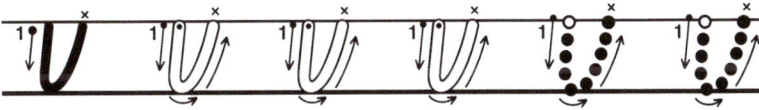

Let's start to read: each word begins with 'V'.

| Vase | Van | Vegetables |

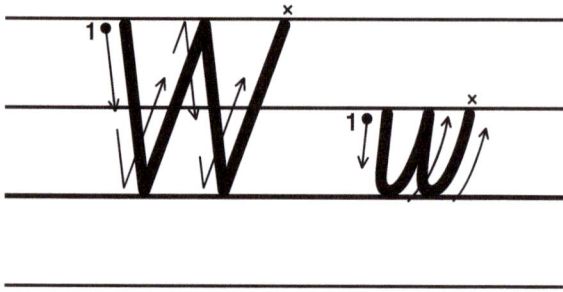

Ww for wind

Let's start to read: each word begins with 'W'.

Worm	Whale	Watermelon

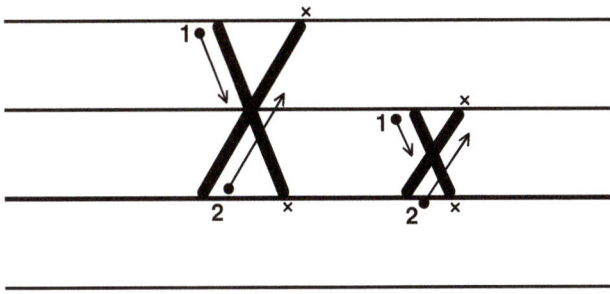

Xx for xylophone

Let's practice. Trace and write the letters.

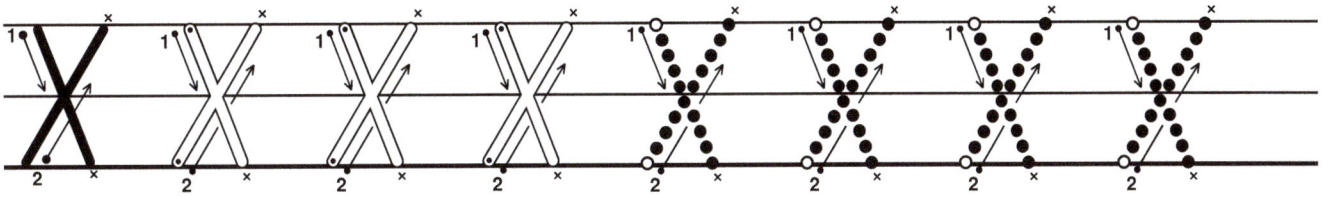

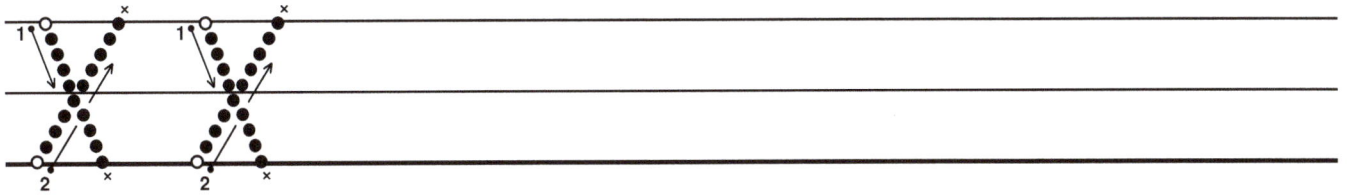

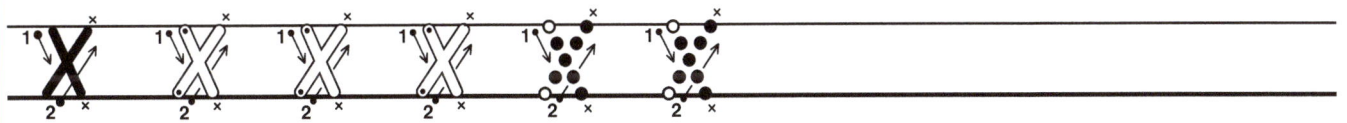

Let's start to read: each word begins with 'X'.

X-ray	Xerus	Xiphias

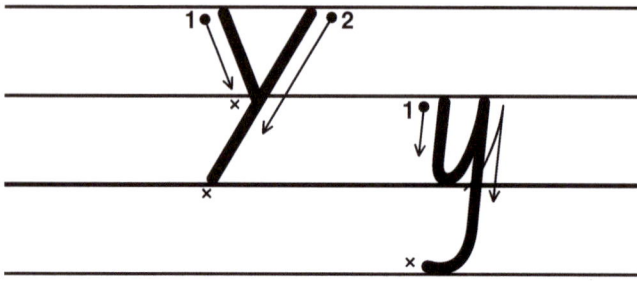

Yy for yo-yo

Let's practice. Trace and write the letters.

Let's start to read: each word begins with 'Y'.

Yak	Yellow	Yacht

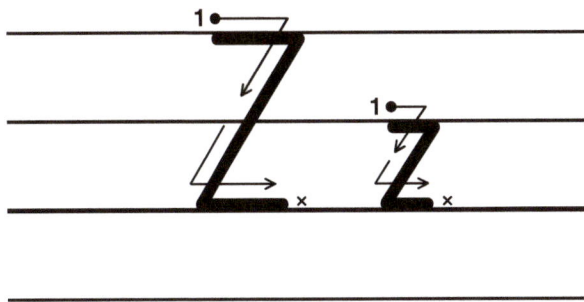

Zz for zoo

Let's practice. Trace and write the letters.

Let's start to read: each word begins with 'Z'.

Zipper	Zebra	Zucchini

Join the upper case and lower case letters to the correct picture.

U

z

V

x

W

u

X

y

Y

w

Z

v

How did you do? Colour the stars to show how well you did.

Look at each of the pictures below and circle the letter that each picture begins with.

u W x

v Y Z

V z w

y X u

Z v U

Y z x

Y w X

W v u

How did you do? Colour the stars to show how well you did.

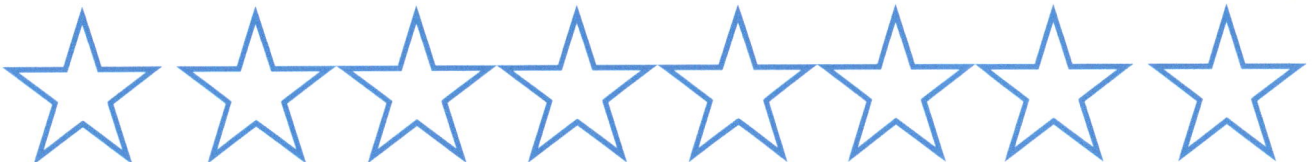

Find the hidden word. Using the pictures, write the correct letter in the boxes below.

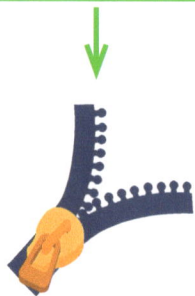

The hidden word is ....? Hint???

The hidden word is ....? Hint???

How did you do? Colour the stars to show how well you did.

Let's practice. Trace and write the letters.

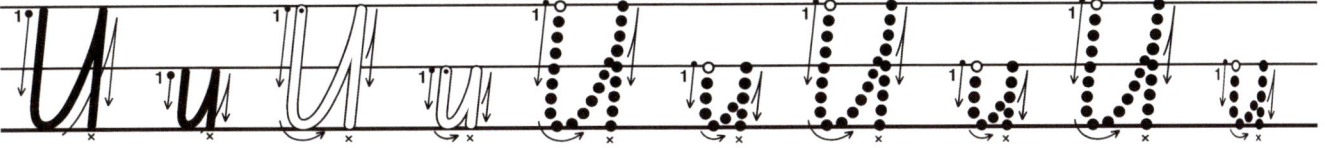

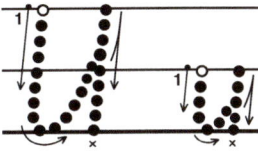

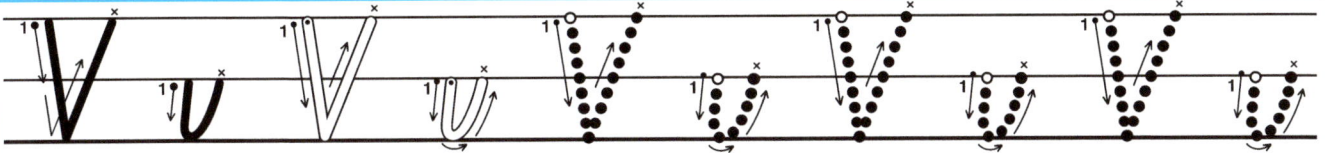

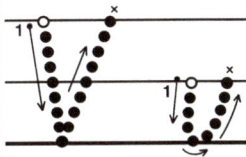

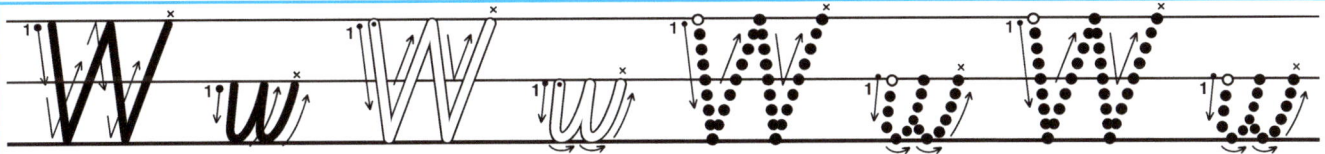

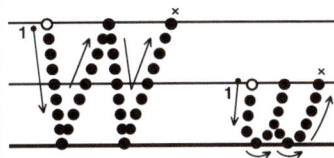

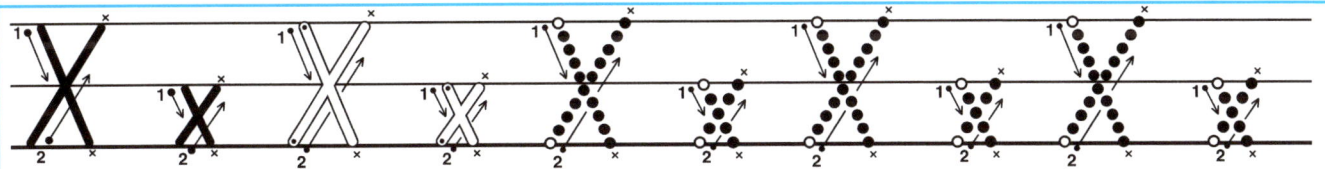

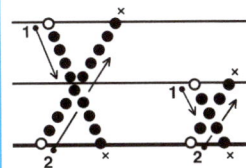

Let's practice. Trace and write the letters.

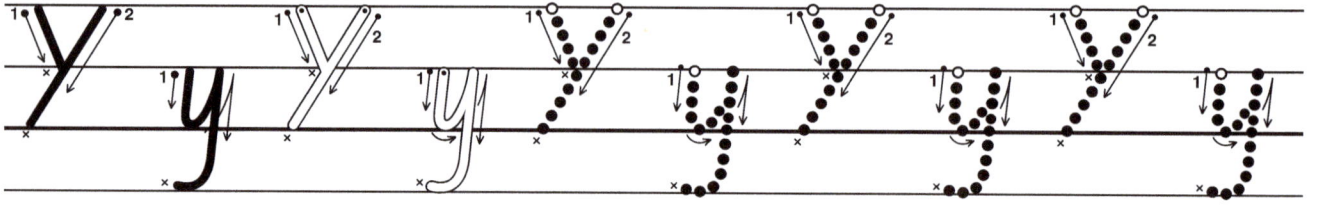

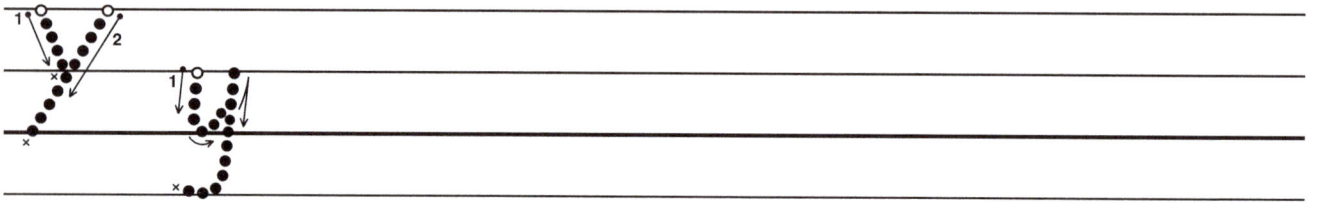

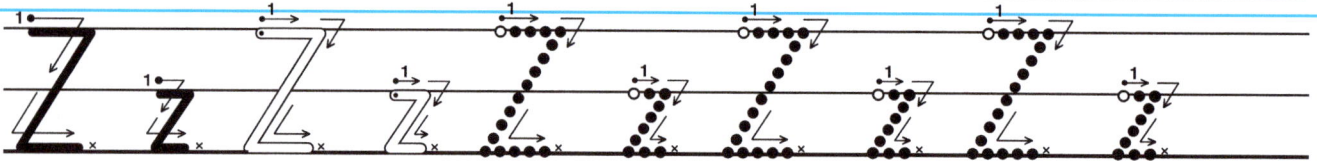

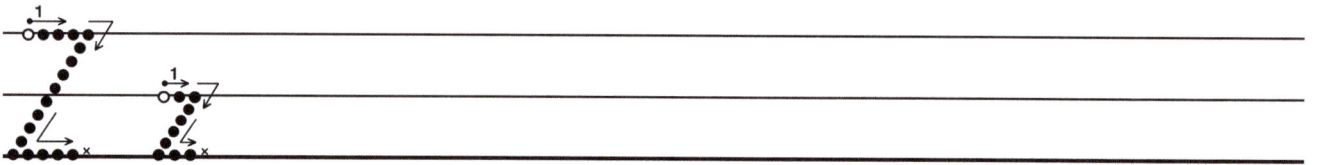

www.ingramcontent.com/pod-product-compliance
Lightning Source LLC
LaVergne TN
LVHW072052070426
835508LV00002B/60